SEW a MODERN HOME

SEW a MODERN HOME

QUILTS AND MORE FOR EVERY ROOM

Melissa Lunden

Martingale®
Create with Confidence

DEDICATION

To my favorite people ever, David and Lila.

>>

Sew a Modern Home: Quilts and More for Every Room
© 2014 by Melissa Lunden

Martingale®
19021 120th Ave. NE, Ste. 102
Bothell, WA 98011-9511 USA
ShopMartingale.com

Printed in China
19 18 17 16 15 14   8 7 6 5 4 3 2 1

**Library of Congress Cataloging-in-Publication Data
is available upon request.**

ISBN: 978-1-60468-367-7

CREDITS

PRESIDENT AND CEO: Tom Wierzbicki

EDITOR IN CHIEF: Mary V. Green

DESIGN DIRECTOR: Paula Schlosser

MANAGING EDITOR: Karen Costello Soltys

ACQUISITIONS EDITOR: Karen M. Burns

TECHNICAL EDITOR: Laurie Baker

COPY EDITOR: Marcy Heffernan

PRODUCTION MANAGER: Regina Girard

COVER AND INTERIOR DESIGNER: Adrienne Smitke

PHOTOGRAPHER: Brent Kane

ILLUSTRATOR: Christine Erikson

*Special thanks to Suzie and Bernhard Bauer
of Snohomish, Washington, for generously allowing
us to photograph in their home.*

ACKNOWLEDGMENTS

This book is a dream come true for me, and it could not have happened without the help of many really amazing people. First of all, I would like to thank everyone at Martingale, especially Karen Burns for sending me that fateful email and Cathy Reitan for all of her patient answers to my never-ending questions. I would also like to thank Laurie Baker, Marcy Heffernan, and Sheila Ryan for all their hard editorial work and fabulous attention to detail. Thank you to Paula Schlosser and Adrienne Smitke for making this book so lovely.

Also a huge thanks to Cynthia Mann and everyone at Birch Fabrics, whose unconditional support and amazing fabrics are what got me here in the first place. Birch also generously donated fabric for many of the projects in this book. I am eternally grateful to have such wonderful fabric to work with. It is a constant source of inspiration to me.

Also, special thanks to Lori Stollmeyer and Alison Verge at The Cotton Ball for letting me take over their long-arm machine. I am so proud of the quilting on these quilts, and it could not have happened without their generosity.

Thank you to all my friends and family who have been so encouraging and supportive to me over the years and particularly during this process. There is no way I could thank all of my great friends and loved ones who were so good to me while I wrote this book, but I promise I'll thank you in person. A giant thank-you and hug go out to Carol Lunden, Nicole Lunden, Samantha Remeika, Dan Sharp, Lily Sharp, and Steve Sharp.

And finally, none of this would have happened without the unconditional and endless love, support, and encouragement of David Sharp.

CONTENTS

INTRODUCTION

>>>

I love sewing things. There's nothing I enjoy more than the challenge of trying something new, the rush of creativity, the pleasure of giving a gift, and the pride in finishing something amazing. Because of that, sewing has changed me for the better. It's taught me patience and precision and allowed me to embrace a creative side of myself that I didn't know existed. It has also taught me the phrase, *"I can do that."*

Recently I noticed that my love of interior design and my love of quilting were fusing together in a marvelous way. I was falling in love with rugs and tile patterns that could be turned into quilt patterns. I was seeing ways to beautify my home everywhere I looked. The fusion is driven by my desire to make my home as beautiful as possible and to be an active part of the process. Mixing a variety of decor with handmade items allows me to truly create my own perfect domestic space. It's the satisfaction of seeing my own designs and creations fill my home that brings me the most joy.

Some of my favorite projects are compiled within the pages of this book. They're things that I want to see around my house and to give as gifts, designed with the idea that they can work with any taste or style. These projects are for those who are inspired by design, but won't be satisfied unless they make the things themselves in their own unique way.

If you're eager to take inspiration from the world and use it to create your own perfect domestic space, this book is for you. The quilting projects are transitional, appealing to both the modern and more traditional quilter. The designs also are created for a wide array of tastes, with the intention that they appeal to both men and women.

This book is arranged room by room, starting with the living room. A twist on the ever-popular chevron makes for a perfect accent throw quilt.

It pairs gorgeously with chevron starburst and Drunkard's Path pillows, which are bound to make any room pop.

The dining room has three projects that will work on every table. I incorporated traditional flying geese into a table runner, place mats, and napkins. In the spirit of integrating design and function, the table runner uses insulated batting, so hot dishes can be placed right on it. The napkins also have a fun little "quillow" detail, so each one can be folded into itself to create a charming pocket for holding the silverware.

The bedroom quilts aren't too fussy, just simple, versatile designs that will work with any color palette. The main bedroom's quilt is designed around the soothing colors of the desert. The guest-room quilt would also be perfect for your beach house—the one by the sea or the one still on your wish list. The girl's quilt is inspired by my daughter's deep love of the color pink and the stash of pink scraps I had been saving for her. The boy's quilt is strong and graphic, perfect for both easy- and hard-to-please boys.

The nursery section is designed for both expectant parents and gift makers alike. This book will provide instructions to make custom sheets, a crib quilt that embraces both the traditional and the modern, original soft toys, and a whimsical play mat.

Even the outdoor area is covered. The backyard projects, including a picnic quilt and tote bag, are fun extensions of one's home and personal style.

No matter what areas you intend to decorate, the projects are suitable for both beginners and more advanced sewists and quilters. Whichever category you fall into, be sure to read through the basic sewing and quilting information (page 11) to be sure you understand the terms and techniques I use throughout the book. And remember, you can do it!

BASIC INSTRUCTIONS

>>>

It never hurts to go over a few basics, just to be sure we're all on the same page. Everyone has her (or his) own way of doing things, so if you have a different technique that works for you, that's great.

SUPPLIES

In addition to your sewing machine, you'll need the following supplies to make your sewing and quilting experiences enjoyable.

> Good-quality, 100% cotton thread in a neutral color or a color that matches your fabric
> Scissors for cutting fabric and paper
> Rotary cutter, self-healing cutting mat, and acrylic rulers, including a 24"-long ruler for cutting strips and a large square ruler for squaring up blocks and quilt tops as needed
> Fine straight pins
> Fabric-marking pen or pencil

TERMS TO KNOW

Grain lines indicate the direction of the threads that make up the fabric. The *lengthwise grain* runs parallel to the selvage edge and has very little stretch. Cut pieces along the lengthwise grain if they're longer than the width of your fabric. The *crosswise grain* runs from selvage edge to selvage edge. *Bias* is the diagonal line that intersects the lengthwise and crosswise threads, and it stretches the most.

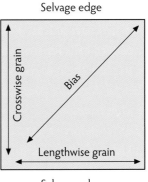

Selvage edges run the lengthwise grain of the fabric and are more tightly woven than the rest of the fabric to keep it from fraying when it's on the loom. Remove the selvage from any pieces that will be included in your project.

Squaring up is often necessary to even out the edges of blocks and quilts and ensure their corners are square (at a 90° angle). If you pay careful attention to your seam allowance and make sure that each piece is cut and sewn accurately, you may not need to square up anything. But, if you find the edges of your block are uneven, use your rotary cutter and ruler to square up the block before assembling your quilt; otherwise you'll end up squaring up your quilt top, and that's a little more difficult, purely because it's larger.

Templates are made by tracing the pattern in the book onto another material, such as paper, pattern material, or template plastic. If the pattern includes a grain-line arrow or other markings, they should be transferred to the template. Cut out the template with scissors that you *don't* use for cutting fabric. When you place the template on the fabric, align the grain-line arrow with the lengthwise or crosswise grain or as specified in the project instructions.

FABRIC

The width of the fabric is measured from selvage edge to selvage edge. Most fabrics are between 43" and 44" wide, but by the time you allow for inconsistencies in width between manufacturers, cut off the selvage edges of the fabric, and allow for shrinkage if you prewash your fabrics, it's safest to assume that you'll have at least 42" of usable fabric. If your pattern calls for strips over 42" wide, you may need to piece them together to achieve the required length. Measure your strip first; your fabric may be wide enough.

Iron your fabrics before you cut them to eliminate wrinkles and foldlines; this will allow you to cut your pieces accurately.

SEAM ALLOWANCES

Unless otherwise instructed, use a ¼"-wide seam allowance when sewing pieces together and press the seam allowances open. Seam allowances have been added to the pattern pieces.

SEWING DIAGONAL EDGES

I love sewing pieces on the diagonal to create designs like chevrons and zigzags (see "Dancing Chevrons Quilt" on page 17). I keep coming back to these designs on a regular basis. There is a trick to sewing the angles, but it's so easy, and once you learn it, it becomes second nature. When sewing two pieces cut on an angle, offset the pieces ¼". That's all there is to it! It may take a little practice to get the right feel for just how much you need to shift your pieces, depending on sewing and fabric variations, but once you get the knack of it, the edges will line up every time.

1. Lay the top piece over the bottom piece and offset the edges ¼".

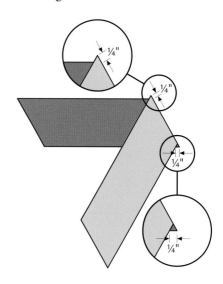

2. After sewing about 1", stop sewing and flip over the top piece to see if the top edges line up. If they do, continue sewing the seam. If they don't, rip out your stitches and readjust the position of the top piece.

SEAM FINISHES

Several projects in this book call for finished seams, including the crib skirt and crib sheet. Seam allowances are finished to secure the raw edges so they don't fray and weaken the seam. There are several different ways to finish a seam.

Pink

Using pinking shears to create a zigzag edge on your seam allowances is a quick and easy way to prevent the threads from fraying. Sew your seam and then pink the edges.

Zigzag Stitch

Another option is to sew a narrow zigzag stitch close to the seam line and then trim the seam allowances close to the zigzag stitching.

Serge

Sergers, or overlock machines, are a great investment for avid sewists, and they're fantastic for finishing a seam. A serger sews the seam, overcasts the edges, and trims the excess fabric all at the same time.

Flat Fell

This is my personal favorite way of finishing a seam. The flat-felled seam involves trimming one seam allowance, folding the other over the trimmed seam allowance, and then securing it with another seam. It makes for a professional look and very secure seam.

1. With *wrong* sides together, sew your pieces together using a ½" seam allowance. (The projects that call for flat-felled seams allow for these wider seam allowances in their cutting instructions.) Press the seam allowances open and then to one side.

2. Carefully trim the bottom layer of the seam allowance to ⅛".

3. Fold the wider seam allowance over the narrower seam allowance so the raw edge meets the seam; press. Stitch along the folded edge.

HAND STITCHING

Sometimes, finishing a piece calls for a bit of hand sewing for a "seamless" look. The ladder stitch is one of my favorite hand stitches for sewing the folds of two pieces of fabric together. I use it for hand sewing pillows closed when I want them to look seamless. I also use this stitch for attaching binding to quilts, using the backing as the second fold.

To make the ladder stitch, run the needle along the inside of the first fabric fold about ¼". Bring the needle out of the fold and insert it into the fold of the second piece of fabric directly across from where you came out of the first fold. Run the needle under the fold about ¼". Bring it out of the fold and insert it into the fold on the first piece of fabric directly across from where it came out of the second fold. Continue in this manner until the seam is closed. Make a knot in the thread close to the fabric surface, and then insert the needle into the fold and pop the knot through to the inside. Bring the needle out through the fold and clip the thread close to the fabric surface.

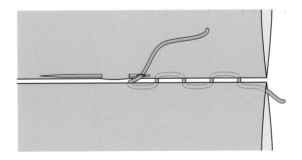

You can vary the stitch length depending on what you're sewing. If you are sewing a stuffed pillow closed, where there's stress on the seam, you'll want your stitches to be very small. If you're sewing a quilt binding, your stitch length can be a bit longer.

QUILT FINISHING

Once your quilt top is finished, you'll need to layer it with batting and backing, quilt the layers together, and then bind the quilt edges.

Assembling the Layers

Follow these steps if you're hand or machine quilting your project. If you plan to use the services of a long-arm machine quilter, check with your quilter before proceeding.

1. Cut and piece your backing, if necessary, so it is at least 3" longer and 3" wider than the quilt top on each side. Press the backing, and then lay it on your work surface wrong side up.

2. Using painter's tape or masking tape, tape the backing to your work surface in the center of each side and the four corners. The quilt backing should be flat and slightly taut but not stretched.

3. Position the quilt batting over the quilt backing. Smooth out any wrinkles. The batting should cling to the fabric.

4. Center the quilt top, right side up, over the batting. Smooth out any wrinkles.

5. If you're hand quilting, thread baste the layers together, working from the center outward. If you're machine quilting, pin baste with size 1 rustproof safety pins. Small quilts can also be basted together with temporary spray adhesive.

6. Quilt the layers together by hand or machine. Start quilting from the center and work your way out toward the edges. This will help prevent puckering or shifting of the quilt layers.

7. After you've finished quilting, trim the excess batting and backing and square up your quilt.

Binding the Edges

1. Sew your 2½"-wide binding strips together at right angles, right sides together. Trim the seam allowances to ¼", and then press the seam allowances open.

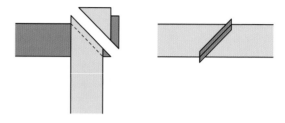

2. Press the binding strip in half lengthwise, wrong sides together.

3. Position the end of the binding at about the midway point on one edge of the quilt top, aligning the raw edges. Start sewing about 10" from the end of the binding, using a ¼" seam allowance. Stop sewing ¼" from the first corner. Backstitch, clip the threads, and remove the quilt from the machine.

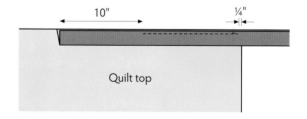

4. Rotate the quilt so you're ready to sew the next side. Fold the binding straight up at a 90° angle away from the quilt. Keeping the angled edge intact, fold the binding back down onto itself so the binding raw edge is aligned with the quilt raw edge. Start stitching ¼" from the corner with a backstitch and continue sewing until you are ¼" from the next corner. Continue sewing the binding to the edges of the quilt, repeating the folding and stitching process at each corner.

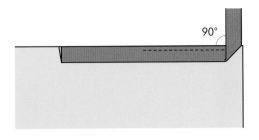

5. Stop sewing and backstitch when you're about 5" from the beginning of the binding.

6. Overlap the end of the strip with the beginning of the strip. Cut off the excess end so the binding-strip ends overlap 2½".

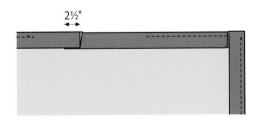

7. Open up both ends of the binding strip and place the ends right sides together at right angles. Pin the ends together and then mark the seam line between the points where the strips intersect. Sew the binding together on the marked line. Trim the excess fabric, leaving a ¼"-wide seam allowance. Press the seam allowances open.

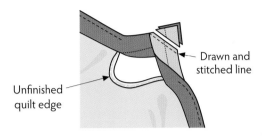

8. Refold the binding in half and continue stitching the binding in place.

9. Flip the binding over the raw edge of the quilt and either machine stitch it to the back of the quilt or hand stitch it to the back of the quilt using a ladder stitch, mitering the corners as you come to them.

living room

Gorgeous living-room accessories are the easiest way to make your room shine. These projects are versatile and work with any decor, making the living room your favorite room in the house.

DANCING CHEVRONS QUILT

FINISHED QUILT: 60" x 60½"

Classic colors pair with angled pieces to create this graphic and geometric design. Bind the quilt with a coordinating print in the same color as the accent strips to make it pop. I used Birch Fabrics' Shroom, Cream, and Sun for the quilt top and Knotty Bois Sun for the binding.

MATERIALS

Yardage is based on 42"-wide fabric.

2 yards of gray solid for parallelograms

2 yards of cream solid for parallelograms

⅝ yard of yellow solid for accent strips

⅝ yard of yellow wood-grain print for binding

3¾ yards of fabric for backing

66" x 66" piece of batting

Template plastic

CUTTING

Trace the pattern on page 20 onto template plastic and cut it out. Use the template to cut the A and A reversed pieces.

From the gray solid, cut:
21 strips, 3" x 42"; cut into 42 A and 42 A reversed pieces

From the cream solid, cut:
21 strips, 3" x 42"; cut into 42 A and 42 A reversed pieces

From the yellow solid, cut:
18 strips, 1" x 42"; crosscut into 144 rectangles, 1" x 5"

From the yellow wood-grain print, cut:
7 strips, 2½" x 42"

> ### DOUBLE UP
> Lay two gray strips wrong sides together and you'll be able to cut one A and one A reversed piece at the same time. Do the same with the cream strips.

PIECING THE ROWS

Use ¼"-wide seam allowances and sew with right sides together.

1. Center and sew a yellow 1" x 5" rectangle along one angled end of a gray A piece. Press the seam allowances open. Using a rotary cutter and ruler, trim off the excess ends of the rectangle even with the A piece.

2. Refer to "Sewing Diagonal Edges" (page 12) to sew a cream A piece to the yellow end of the unit from step 1. Press the seam allowances open.

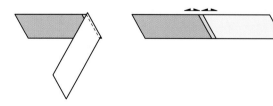

3. Continue adding gray and cream A pieces and yellow 1" x 5" rectangles to the unit from step 2, following the same sequence as in steps 1 and 2 until you've joined a strip with four gray pieces, three cream pieces, and six yellow rectangles.

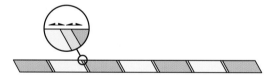

4. Repeat steps 1–3 to make a total of six strips.

5. Repeat steps 1–3 with the gray and cream A reversed pieces and yellow rectangles to make a total of six mirror-image units.

Make 6.

6. Join each strip from step 4 to a strip from step 5 as shown, matching seams. Trim the ends of each strip as shown to create a straight edge.

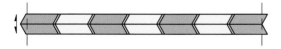

7. Repeat steps 1–6 to make six additional joined rows, alternating the colors so that each row begins and ends with a cream A piece.

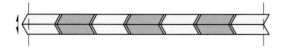

ASSEMBLING THE QUILT TOP

1. Beginning with a strip that starts with a gray A piece, join the strips so that the colors alternate. Make sure that all chevrons are pointing in the same direction as shown below. Press the seam allowances open.

2. Stay stitch the edges of the quilt top.

FINISHING THE QUILT

Refer to "Quilt Finishing" on pages 14 and 15.

1. Piece the quilt backing so it is 6" longer and 6" wider than the quilt top.

2. Layer the quilt top with backing and batting; baste the layers together.

3. Quilt as desired. Quilting suggestion: My quilt was quilted with zigzag lines that echo the yellow rectangles.

4. Square up the quilt sandwich.

5. Bind the quilt with the yellow wood-grain print 2½"-wide strips.

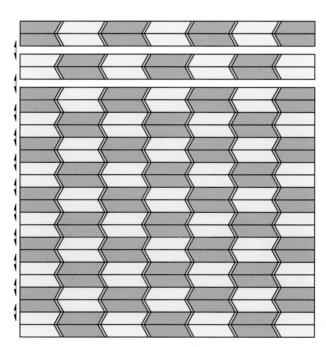

Quilt assembly

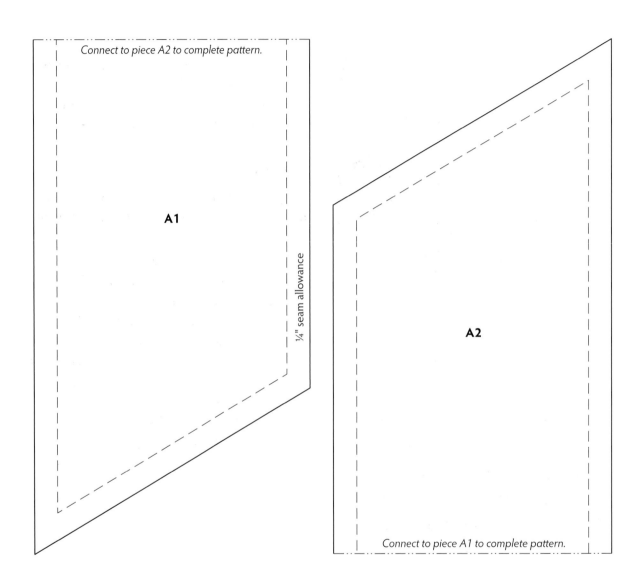

Connect to piece A2 to complete pattern.

A1

¼" seam allowance

A2

Connect to piece A1 to complete pattern.

CHEVRON STARBURST PILLOW

A center square surrounded by larger triangles makes this pillow burst with energy. I used a chevron print, but stripes or other graphic designs would look just as stunning.

MATERIALS

⅔ yard of 54"-wide narrow chevron print home-decor fabric for pillow front

1 fat quarter (18" x 21") of fabric for pillow back

16" x 16" pillow insert or polyester fiberfill

CUTTING

Cut pairs of identical squares from the same area of the print and cut each one in half diagonally in the same direction.

From the chevron print, cut:

2 identical squares, 9½" x 9½"; cut in half diagonally to yield 4 triangles

2 identical squares, 6¾" x 6¾"; cut in half diagonally to yield 4 triangles

2 identical squares, 5" x 5"; cut in half diagonally to yield 4 triangles

1 square, 4½" x 4½"

2 identical squares, 3¾" x 3¾"; cut in half diagonally to yield 4 triangles

From the fat quarter, cut:

1 square, 17" x 17"

MAKING THE PILLOW

Use ¼"-wide seam allowances and sew with right sides together.

1. Fold the 4½" square in half vertically and finger-press the ends to mark the center of the opposite sides. Fold the square in half crosswise and finger-press the ends to mark the centers of the remaining two sides. Fold each triangle in half along the long edge and finger-press the long edge to mark the center.

2. Sew 3¾" triangles to opposite sides of the 4½" square, aligning the center marks. Press the seam allowances open. Trim the sides of the unit ¼" from the points of the center square.

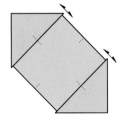
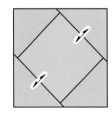

3. Repeat step 2 to add the 5" triangles and then the 6¾" triangles to the unit, trimming ¼" from the points of the previous unit after each round is complete.

4. Sew the 9½" triangles to the sides of the unit from step 3. Trim the sides of the unit ½" from the points of the previous unit.

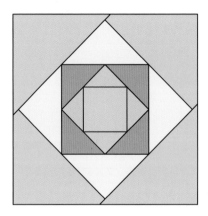

5. Place the pieced front and the backing 17" square right sides together. Using a ½"-wide seam allowance, sew around the edges, leaving a large opening on one side for inserting the pillow form or fiberfill. Clip the corners and turn the pillow cover right side out; push out the corners. Press, pressing the opening seam allowances to the inside.

6. Insert the pillow form into the pillow-cover opening or firmly stuff the pillow with fiberfill. Use a ladder stitch (page 13) to close the opening.

SPIN ME RIGHT ROUND PILLOW

FINISHED PILLOW: 14" x 14"

A modern twist on a Drunkard's Path block pops with four high-contrast colors. The versatile pillow brings movement and energy into any room in your house. This pillow features Birch Fabrics' solids in Sun, Mahogany, Cream, and Shroom.

MATERIALS

Yardage is based on 42"-wide fabric.

¼ yard of dark-brown solid for patchwork

¼ yard of cream solid for patchwork

¼ yard of gray solid for patchwork

¼ yard of yellow solid for patchwork

12" x 12" pillow insert or polyester fiberfill

CUTTING

Trace the patterns on page 25 onto template plastic and cut them out. Use the templates to cut the A and B pieces. Clip each A and B piece where indicated.

From *each* of the solids, cut:

8 A pieces (32 total)

8 B pieces (32 total)

MAKING THE PILLOW

Use ¼"-wide seam allowances and sew with right sides together.

1. Pin the yellow A pieces to the brown B pieces, right sides together, matching the center clips on each pair of pieces.

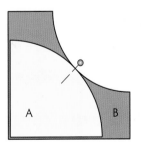

2. Starting at the center clip, with piece B on top, sew one half of the seam allowance, backstitching at the end of the seam. Return to the center and stitch the other half of the seam. You may find it easier to sew if you make small snips, about ⅛" deep, into the seam allowance of piece B. Press the seam allowances toward the A piece. Repeat to make eight of each combination as shown.

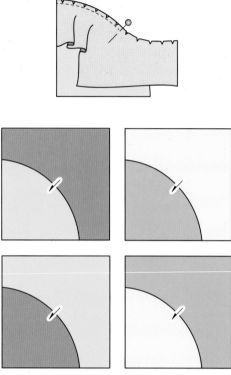

Make 8 of each.

3. Arrange the prepared units as shown above right to form the design. For the pillow front, you'll use the units with yellow A and gray A pieces. For the pillow back, you'll use the units with brown A and cream A pieces. Sew the units together in rows, pressing the seam allowances toward the unit without a seam

intersection or press them open. Sew the rows together. Press.

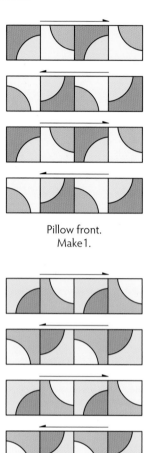

Pillow front.
Make 1.

Pillow back.
Make 1.

4. Sew the pillow front to the pillow back, right sides together, using a ¼"-wide seam allowance and leaving a 5" opening along one edge for turning and stuffing. Clip the corners, turn the pillow cover right side out, and press. Press under ¼" along both edges of the opening.

5. Insert the pillow form into the opening or firmly stuff the pillow with fiberfill. Use a ladder stitch (page 13) to close the opening.

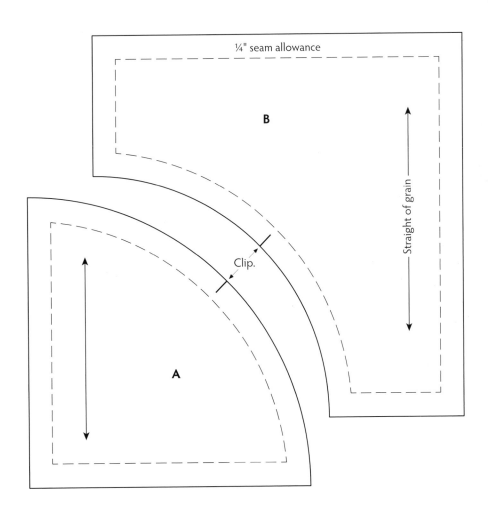

¼" seam allowance

B

Straight of grain

Clip.

A

dining room

The flying-geese design used for this dining-room collection is timeless, classic, and incredibly versatile. I picked some of my favorite colors in linen, but these designs could easily be made from cotton fabrics and customized for any holiday or season. These projects also make for gorgeous, personal housewarming gifts.

FINISHED PLACE MAT: 16" x 12½"

This quick and easy set of six place mats makes for a gorgeous table. They coordinate perfectly with the napkins and the table runner, but are interesting enough to be used on their own.

MATERIALS

Yardage is based on 42"-wide fabric, and is enough to make six place mats.

2 yards of white solid linen for tops and binding

⅛ yard *each* of dusty-blue, light-blue, dark-gray, navy, rose, and yellow solid linen for flying-geese units

1⅜ yards of fabric for backings

1⅓ yards of batting

CUTTING

From the white solid linen, cut:

2 strips, 12½" x 42"; crosscut into 6 rectangles, 12½" x 13"

11 strips, 2½" x 42"

5 strips, 2" x 42"; crosscut into 96 squares, 2" x 2"

2 strips, 1½" x 42"; crosscut into 6 rectangles, 1½" x 12½"

From *each* of the dusty-blue, light-blue, dark-gray, navy, rose, and yellow solid linens, cut:

8 rectangles, 2" x 3½" (48 total)

From the backing fabric, cut:

3 strips, 15" x 42"; crosscut into 6 rectangles, 15" x 18"

From the batting, cut:

6 rectangles, 15" x 18"

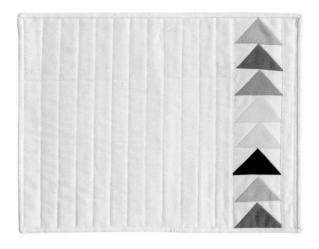

direction as shown. Press the seam allowances open. Make six rows.

Make 6.

MAKING THE PLACE-MAT TOPS

1. Draw a diagonal line on the wrong side of each white 2" square.

2. Position a marked square on one end of a dusty-blue 2" x 3½" rectangle, right sides together. Sew on the marked line. Trim the excess fabric ¼" from the stitching line. Press the seam allowances open. Repeat on the opposite end of the rectangle to make a flying-geese unit. Repeat to make a total of eight dusty-blue flying-geese units.

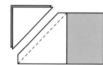

Make 8.

3. Repeat step 2 with the remaining marked white squares and the light-blue, dark-gray, navy, rose, and yellow rectangles to make a total of 48 flying-geese units.

4. Select eight flying-geese units in assorted colors. Sew the units together in a vertical row with all of the units pointing in the same

5. Sew a white 1½" x 12½" rectangle to the right edge of a flying-geese strip. Sew a white 12½" x 13" rectangle to the left edge of the flying-geese strip. Press the seam allowances open.

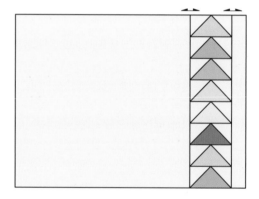

6. Repeat step 5 to make a total of six place-mat tops.

FINISHING THE PLACE MATS

Refer to "Quilt Finishing" on pages 14 and 15.

1. Layer each place-mat top with a batting and backing rectangle; baste the layers together.

2. Quilt as desired. Quilting suggestion: Use the bottom seam of each flying-geese unit as a guide to stitch horizontal lines across the place-mat top, or stitch vertical lines using the short edge of the place mat as a guide.

3. Bind each place mat with the white 2½"-wide strips.

BIRDS OF A FEATHER TABLE RUNNER

FINISHED TABLE RUNNER: 12½" x 44"

This crisp and cheery table runner can easily be adjusted to fit any table by adding additional rows of geese. If you want to add an extra layer of functionality to the runner, use a piece of insulated batting along with the cotton batting when you quilt the runner so that you can put hot serving dishes directly on it without harming your table.

MATERIALS

Yardage is based on 42"-wide fabric.

1 yard of white solid linen for top and binding

⅛ yard *each* of dusty-blue, light-blue, dark-gray, navy, rose, and yellow solid linen for flying-geese units

1½ yards of fabric for backing

16" x 47" piece of cotton batting

16" x 47" piece of insulated batting (optional)

CUTTING

From the white solid linen, cut:
1 strip, 12½" x 42"; crosscut into:
    3 rectangles, 6½" x 12½"
    2 rectangles, 3¼" x 12½"
    2 rectangles, 1½" x 12½"
5 strips, 2" x 42"; crosscut into 96 squares, 2" x 2"
3 strips, 2½" x 42"

From *each* of the dusty-blue, light-blue, dark-gray, navy, rose, and yellow solid linens, cut:
8 rectangles, 2" x 3½" (48 total)

PIECING THE TABLE RUNNER

1. Refer to steps 1–4 of "Making the Place-Mat Tops" (page 28) to make six vertical rows of flying-geese units.

2. Refer to the table-runner assembly diagram at right to arrange the flying-geese strips and the remaining white-solid rectangles as shown. Sew the pieces together. Press the seam allowances open.

FINISHING THE TABLE RUNNER

Refer to "Quilt Finishing" on pages 14 and 15.

1. Piece the table-runner backing so it is 3" longer and 3" wider than the table-runner top.

2. Layer the table-runner top with backing and cotton batting. If you're using the insulated batting, layer it between the cotton batting and the table-runner top, reflective side up. Baste the layers together.

3. Quilt as desired. Quilting suggestion: In the white sections, quilt straight lines parallel to the flying-geese strips.

4. Square up the table-runner sandwich.

5. Bind the table runner with the white 2½"-wide strips.

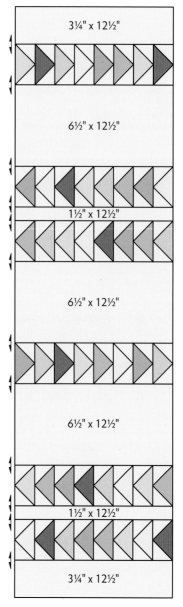

Table-runner assembly

FLYING GEESE NAPKINS

These napkins are a fun twist on the "quillow" concept of tucking a quilt into an attached pocket to make a pillow. I couldn't resist adding a sweet little pocket. By having it match the color of the napkin, it's very subtle when unfolded. When folded, the flying-geese pocket is revealed and creates a fun way to set your table with the silverware tucked into the pocket.

MATERIALS

Yardage is based on 42"-wide fabric and is enough to make six napkins.

2⅛ yards of dusty-blue solid linen for napkins and pockets

⅛ yard of white solid linen for flying-geese units

CUTTING

From the dusty-blue solid linen, cut:

3 strips, 18" x 42"; crosscut into 6 squares 18" x 18"

1 strip, 2" x 42"; crosscut into:

    12 squares, 2" x 2"

    12 rectangles, 1½" x 2"

1 strip, 5½" x 42"; crosscut into 6 rectangles, 5½" x 6"

1 strip, 2" x 42"; crosscut into 6 rectangles, 2" x 5½"

From the white solid linen, cut:

6 rectangles, 2" x 3½"

MAKING THE POCKETS

1. Draw a diagonal line on the wrong side of each blue 2" square. Position a marked square on one end of a white 2" x 3½" rectangle, right sides together. Sew on the marked line. Trim the excess fabric ¼" from the stitching line. Press the seam allowances open. Repeat, sewing a blue square on the opposite end of the rectangle to make a flying-geese unit. Repeat to make a total of six flying-geese units.

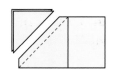
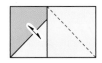

Make 6.

2. Sew blue 1½" x 2" rectangles to the sides of a flying-geese unit. Press the seam allowances open. Repeat to make a total of six units.

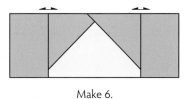

Make 6.

3. Sew a blue 2" x 5½" rectangle to the bottom of a flying-geese unit from step 2 and a blue 5½" x 6" rectangle to the top. Press the seam allowances open. Repeat to make a total of six units.

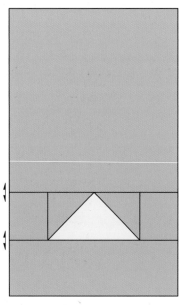

Make 6.

4. Fold a unit from step 3 in half as shown above right, aligning the raw edges. Stitch the raw edges together, leaving a 2" opening along the bottom edge for turning. Clip the corners and turn the pocket right side out. Push out the corners. Press, pressing the seam allowances along the opening to the inside.

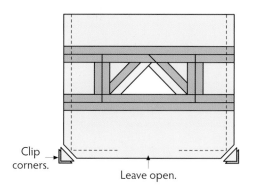

Clip corners.

Leave open.

5. Topstitch across the top of the pocket.

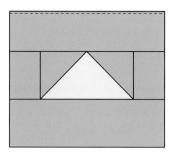

6. Repeat steps 4 and 5 with the remaining flying-geese units from step 3 to make a total of six pockets.

MAKING THE NAPKINS

1. Press each corner of a blue 18" square to the wrong side ¾". Trim the excess corner fabric ¼" from the fold.

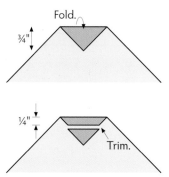

Fold.

¾"

¼"

Trim.

2. Press the sides of the square to the wrong side ¼". Press the sides to the wrong side another ¼", mitering the corners.

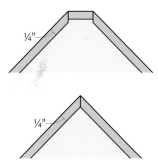

3. Sew along the inner fabric fold around the entire square to complete the hem.

4. Lay the napkin right side up on your work surface. Mark the center point of the bottom edge of the napkin. Position the flying-geese pocket face down on the napkin, lining up the right edge of the pocket with the napkin center mark as shown. The point of the flying-geese unit should be pointing toward the top edge. Stitch the pocket to the napkin along the left, bottom, and right edges, backstitching at the beginning and end to secure the pocket.

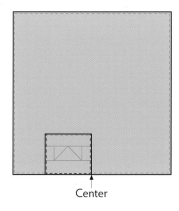

Center

5. Repeat steps 1–4 for all six napkins

FOLDING THE NAPKINS

1. Turn the napkin over so the pocket is face down. Fold the edges toward the center, aligning the right-hand fold with the pocket seam line. Fold the napkin in half vertically.

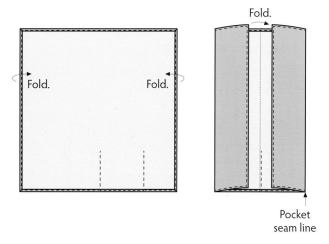

Fold.

Fold.   Fold.

Pocket seam line

2. Fold the napkin in half horizontally.

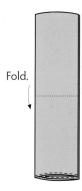

Fold.

3. Turn the pocket to the right side, enclosing the napkin finished edges. Push out the pocket corners.

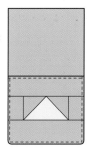

4. Repeat steps 1–3 with the remaining napkins and pockets.

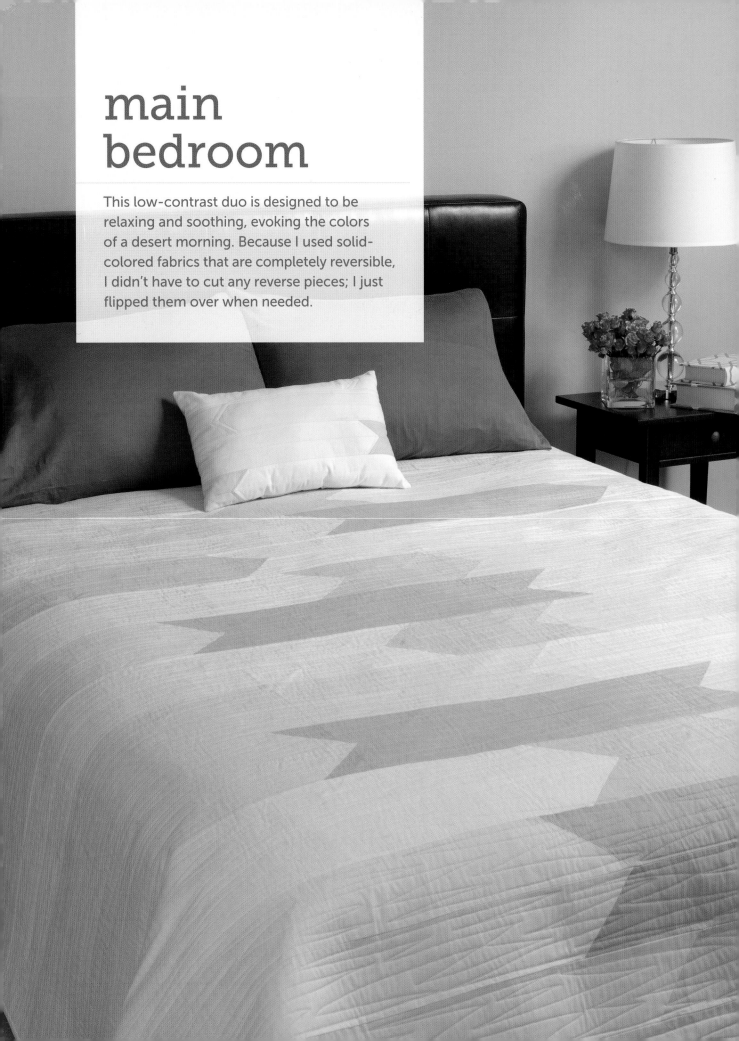

main bedroom

This low-contrast duo is designed to be relaxing and soothing, evoking the colors of a desert morning. Because I used solid-colored fabrics that are completely reversible, I didn't have to cut any reverse pieces; I just flipped them over when needed.

DESERT MORNING QUILT

FINISHED QUILT: 84½" x 84½"

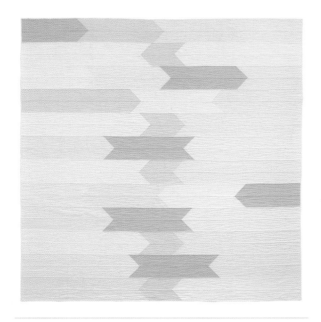

This quilt is made from six pastel solids sewn into a dozen pairs of strips, each making a combination of chevrons. Three different strip combinations alternate to create the abstract design. The chevrons are created by cutting the strip ends at 45° angles, so cutting the pieces is easy to do with standard rotary-cutting equipment.

MATERIALS

Yardage is based on 42"-wide fabric.

2½ yards of off-white solid for chevron strips

1¾ yards of pale-pink solid for chevron strips and binding

1¾ yards of pale-peach solid for chevron strips

1½ yards of gray solid for chevron strips

1⅛ yards of beige solid for chevron strips

1 yard of tan solid for chevron strips

7⅝ yards of fabric for backing

91" x 93" piece of batting

CUTTING

Cut all strips along the lengthwise grain unless otherwise indicated.

From the gray solid, cut:
6 pieces, 4" x 28" (F)
2 pieces, 4" x 27" (B)
4 pieces, 4" x 21¼" (A)

From the off-white solid, cut:
12 pieces, 4" x 39¼" (C)
2 pieces, 4" x 28" (F)
2 pieces, 4" x 27" (B)
2 pieces, 4" x 21¼" (A)

From the tan solid, cut:
2 pieces, 4" x 36½" (E)
2 pieces, 4" x 27" (B)
10 pieces, 4" x 14" (D)

From the pale-pink solid, cut:
6 pieces, 4" x 28" (G)
2 pieces, 4" x 27" (B)
4 pieces, 4" x 21¼" (A)

Continued on page 36

PIECING THE QUILT TOP

1. Referring to the cutting list for the piece letters and colors, cut the ends of the pieces at a 45° angle as shown.

**Pieces A and
A reversed**
Make 2 each from gray
and pink. Make 1 each
from off-white and peach.

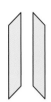

**Pieces B and
B reversed**
Make 1 each from peach,
tan, pink, gray, beige,
and off-white.

**Pieces C and
C reversed**
Make 6 each from off-white.
Make 4 each from peach.

**Pieces D and
D reversed**
Make 5 each from tan.

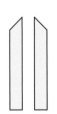

**Pieces E and
E reversed**
Make 3 each from beige.
Make 1 each from tan.

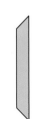

Piece F
Make 6 from gray.
Make 2 from off-white.

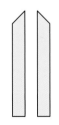

**Pieces G and
G reversed**
Make 3 each from pink.
Make 1 each from beige.

Continued from page 35

**From the *crosswise grain* of the remaining
pale-pink solid, cut:**
9 strips, 2½" x 42" (binding)

From the pale-peach solid, cut:
8 pieces, 4" x 39¼" (C)
2 pieces, 4" x 27" (B)
2 pieces, 4" x 21¼" (A)

From the beige solid, cut:
6 pieces, 4" x 36½" (E)
2 pieces, 4" x 28" (G)
2 pieces, 4" x 27" (B)

2. Arrange the pieces in 24 horizontal rows as shown in the quilt assembly diagram below. Refer to "Sewing Diagonal Edges" (page 12) to join the pieces in each row. Press the seam allowances open. Sew the rows together in pairs, and then sew the pairs together. Press the seam allowances open.

FINISHING THE QUILT

Refer to "Quilt Finishing" on pages 14 and 15.

1. Piece the quilt backing so it is 6" longer and 6" wider than the quilt top.

2. Layer the quilt top with backing and batting; baste the layers together.

3. Quilt as desired. Quilting suggestion: I quilted this with a wide free-motion zigzag design.

4. Square up the quilt sandwich.

5. Bind the quilt with the pale-pink 2½"-wide strips.

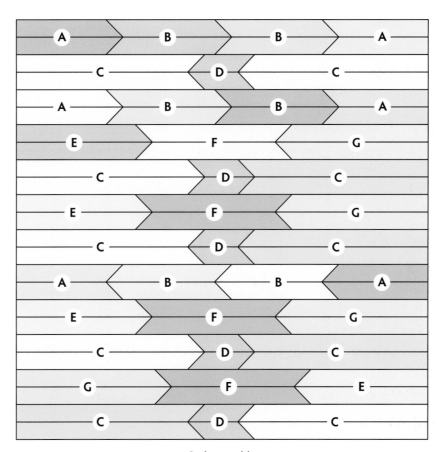

Quilt assembly

DESERT MORNING PILLOW

FINISHED PILLOW: 18" x 11½"

This subtle and soothing pillow pairs gorgeously with the "Desert Morning Quilt." The low-contrast colors are perfect for relaxing and getting a good night's rest.

MATERIALS

Yardage is based on 42"-wide fabric.

¼ yard of off-white solid for chevron strips

1 fat eighth (9" x 21") of pale-pink solid for chevron strips

1 fat eighth of beige solid for chevron strips

5" x 6" piece of pale-peach solid for chevron strips

5" x 6" piece of tan solid for chevron strips

5" x 6" piece of gray solid for chevron strips

½ yard of fabric for pillow back

½ yard of batting

Cotton or polyester fiberfill

CUTTING

From the off-white solid, cut:
4 pieces, 2" x 16½"

From the tan solid, cut:
2 pieces, 2" x 5"

From the gray solid, cut:
2 pieces, 2" x 5"

From the pale-pink solid, cut:
2 pieces, 2" x 16½"
2 pieces, 2" x 5"

From the beige solid, cut:
2 pieces, 2" x 16½"

From the pale-peach solid, cut:
2 pieces, 2" x 5"

From the batting, cut:
2 rectangles, 13" x 20"

From the pillow-back fabric, cut:
1 rectangle, 13" x 20"

ASSEMBLING THE PILLOW TOP

1. Cut the ends of each off-white, tan, gray, pale-pink, beige, and pale-peach piece at a 45° angle as shown.

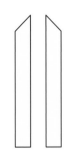

Make 2 each from off-white. Make 1 each from pink and beige.

Make 1 each from tan, gray, pink, beige, and peach.

2. Arrange the pieces in eight horizontal rows as shown. Refer to "Sewing Diagonal Edges" (page 12) to join the pieces in each row. Press the seam allowances open. Sew the rows together in pairs, and then sew the pairs together. Press the seam allowances open.

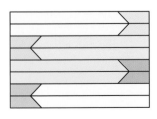

FINISHING THE PILLOW

Refer to "Quilt Finishing" on pages 14 and 15.

1. Layer the pillow front with a batting rectangle; baste the layers together. Repeat with the pillow back and batting rectangles.

2. Quilt the front and back as desired. Trim the batting even with the pillow front. It should measure 19" x 12½". Trim the quilted pillow back to 19" x 12½".

3. Place the front and back pieces right sides together. Using a ½"-wide seam allowance, sew around the edges, leaving a 6" opening on one long side to insert the fiberfill. Clip the corners and turn the pillow cover right side out; push out the corners. Press, pressing the opening seam allowances to the inside.

4. Firmly stuff the pillow with fiberfill. Use a ladder stitch (page 13) to close the opening.

guest
bedroom

This quilt and pillow combination are perfect for any guest room where you want your company to feel relaxed and welcome. The clean lines will work with any decor and color palette.

HORIZON LINE QUILT

FINISHED QUILT: 79½" x 85"

This stunning quilt is graphic without a lot of fuss, but it still manages to evoke the feeling of the ocean. Pick your three favorite colors and personalize your guest room—or any bedroom.

MATERIALS

Yardage is based on 42"-wide fabric.

3¼ yards of white solid for stripes and binding

2⅝ yards of dark-teal solid for stripes

2⅝ yards of light-teal solid for stripes

7¼ yards of fabric for backing

86" x 91" piece of batting

CUTTING

From the *crosswise grain* of the white solid, cut:
9 strips, 2½" x 42"

From the *lengthwise grain* of *both* the dark-teal and the remaining white solid, cut:
1 strip, 8½" x 85" (2 total)
1 strip, 7½" x 85" (2 total)
1 strip, 6½" x 85" (2 total)
1 strip, 5½" x 85" (2 total)
1 strip, 4½" x 85" (2 total)
1 strip, 3½" x 85" (2 total)
1 strip, 2½" x 85" (2 total)
1 strip, 1½" x 85" (2 total)

From the *lengthwise grain* of the light-teal solid, cut:
7 strips, 1½" x 85"

PIECING THE QUILT TOP

1. Sew the widest dark-teal strip to the narrowest white strip along the long edges. Sew the next-widest dark-teal strip to the next-narrowest white strip. Continue in this manner until you've sewn the widest white strip to the narrowest dark-teal strip. Press all of the seam allowances open.

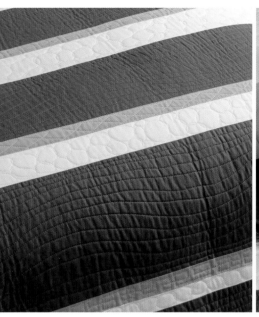

2. Refer to the quilt assembly diagram to lay out the joined strips as shown, inserting a light-teal strip between each of the joined strips. Sew the strips together. Press the seam allowances open.

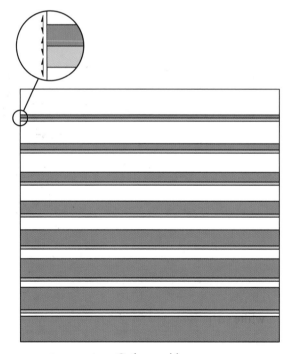

Quilt assembly

FINISHING THE QUILT

Refer to "Quilt Finishing" on pages 14 and 15.

1. Piece the quilt backing so it is 6" longer and 6" wider than the quilt top.

2. Layer the quilt top with backing and batting; baste the layers together.

3. Quilt as desired. Quilting suggestion: I alternated between gentle waves in the dark-teal sections, pebbles in the white sections, and a geometric design in the light-teal sections.

4. Square up the quilt sandwich.

5. Bind the quilt with the white 2½"-wide strips.

HORIZON LINE THROW PILLOW

FINISHED PILLOW: 16" x 12"

This gorgeous, high-contrast pillow pairs perfectly with the "Horizon Line Quilt" but can easily work on its own. Personalize it with your favorite color combinations and this pillow will look lovely in any room in your house.

MATERIALS

Yardage is based on 42"-wide fabric.

¼ yard of dark-teal solid for stripes

¼ yard of white solid for stripes

½ yard of light-teal solid for stripes and pillow back

16" x 12" pillow insert or polyester fiberfill

CUTTING

From *both* the dark-teal and white solids, cut:

1 strip, 2¼" x 17" (2 total)

1 strip, 2" x 17" (2 total)

1 strip, 1½" x 17" (2 total)

2 strips, 1" x 17" (4 total)

From the light teal, cut:

4 strips, 1" x 17"

1 rectangle, 12½" x 16½"

MAKING THE PILLOW

1. Sew the strips together as shown using a ¼"-wide seam allowance. Press the seam allowances to one side.

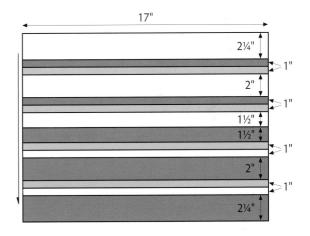

2. Place the pillow front and back right sides together. Using a ½"-wide seam allowance, sew around the edges, leaving a 10" opening on one long side. (If you're using fiberfill, you can shorten the opening by a few inches.) Clip the corners and turn the pillow cover right side out; push out the corners. Press, pressing the opening seam allowances to the inside.

3. Stuff the pillow firmly with fiberfill or insert a pillow form. Use a ladder stitch (page 13) to close the opening.

girl's room

This adorable quilt is perfect for any little girl. It was inspired by a collection of pink scraps that I'd been saving to make my daughter a quilt when she was big enough for a twin bed. Wanting something classic that she wouldn't outgrow too soon, I came up with this design. If pink isn't your girl's favorite color, swap it for assorted scraps in a color that makes her smile.

PINKY PATCH QUILT

FINISHED QUILT: 68" x 84" | FINISHED BLOCK: 12½" x 12½"

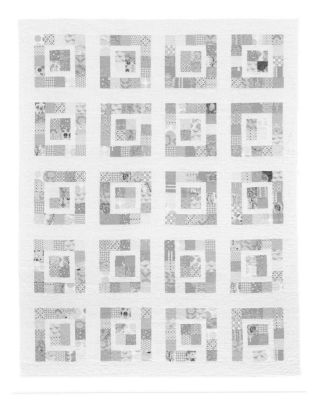

MATERIALS

Yardage is based on 42"-wide fabric.

3¾ yards of white solid for blocks, sashing, border, and binding

3 yards *total* of assorted pink-print scraps for blocks

5½ yards of fabric for backing

74" x 90" piece of batting

CUTTING

From the assorted pink-print scraps, cut a *total* of:
400 squares, 3" x 3"

From the white solid, cut:
20 strips, 4" x 42"; crosscut *9 of the strips* into
    25 rectangles, 4" x 13"
8 strips, 2½" x 42"
14 strips, 1¾" x 42"; crosscut into:
    40 rectangles, 1¾" x 8"
    40 rectangles, 1¾" x 5½"

MAKING THE BLOCKS

Use ¼"-wide seam allowances and press seam allowances open.

1. Select four different pink squares and arrange them in two rows of two squares each. Sew the squares in each row together; press. Sew the rows together; press. Repeat to make a total of 20 center units.

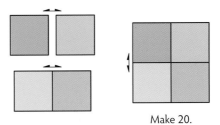

Make 20.

2. Sew white 1¾" x 5½" rectangles to the sides of each center unit; press. Join white 1¾" x 8" rectangles to the top and bottom of each center unit; press.

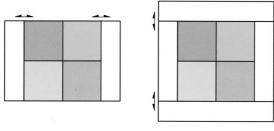

Make 20.

3. Select three different pink squares and sew them together side by side to make a strip; press. Repeat to make a total of 40 side strips. Select five different pink squares and sew them together side by side to make a strip; press. Repeat to make a total of 40 top/bottom strips.

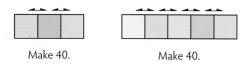

Make 40.   Make 40.

4. Join pieced side strips from step 3 to the sides of each unit from step 2; press. Add pieced top/bottom strips to the top and bottom of each unit to complete the blocks; press.

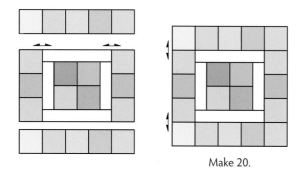

Make 20.

ASSEMBLING THE QUILT TOP

1. Alternately arrange five white 4" x 13" sashing/border strips and four blocks into a horizontal row. Sew the pieces together; press. Repeat to make a total of five block rows.

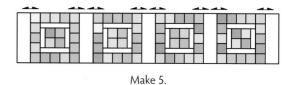

Make 5.

2. Sew the 11 white 4" x 42" strips together end to end to make one long strip; press. Crosscut the pieced strip into six strips, 4" x 68", for the horizontal sashing/border strips.

3. Refer to the quilt assembly diagram to alternately arrange the horizontal sashing/border strips and the block rows. Sew the strips and rows together; press.

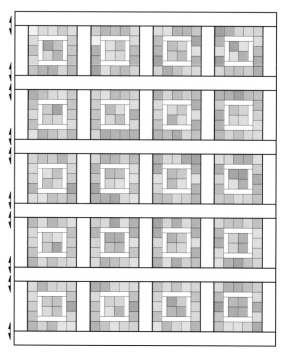

Quilt assembly

FINISHING THE QUILT

Refer to "Quilt Finishing" on pages 14 and 15.

1. Piece the quilt backing so it is 6" longer and 6" wider than the quilt top.

2. Layer the quilt top with backing and batting; baste the layers together.

3. Quilt as desired. Quilting suggestion: I quilted an allover whimsical design of swirls and hearts.

4. Square up the quilt sandwich.

5. Bind the quilt with the white 2½"-wide strips.

boy's room

This quilt is bound to appeal to even the pickiest of boys, and with the simple piecing, it's easy to make a big impact without spending a lot of time. Because the quilt's made up of two large blocks connected with a strip of white fabric, you can sew it up quickly. Customize the quilt by selecting fabrics in the colors of his favorite sports team or switch out a solid fabric for a fun novelty print.

SHARP TURN QUILT

MATERIALS

Yardage is based on 42"-wide fabric.

3¾ yards of white solid for blocks, connecting
   strip, and binding

1 yard of gray solid for blocks

⅞ yard of red solid for blocks

⅝ yard of blue solid for blocks

5½ yards of fabric for backing

68" x 96" piece of batting

CUTTING

From the white solid, cut:

26 strips, 4" x 42"; crosscut *16 of the strips* into:
   2 pieces, 4" x 40"
   2 pieces, 4" x 38½"
   2 pieces, 4" x 34"
   2 pieces, 4" x 32½"
   2 pieces, 4" x 28"
   2 pieces, 4" x 26½"
   2 pieces, 4" x 22"
   2 pieces, 4" x 20½"
   2 pieces, 4" x 18"
   2 pieces, 4" x 16"
   2 pieces, 4" x 10"
   8 strips, 2½" x 42"

From the gray solid, cut:

10 strips, 3" x 42"; crosscut *5 of the strips* into:
   2 pieces, 3" x 36"
   2 pieces, 3" x 24½"
   2 pieces, 3" x 18"
   2 pieces, 3" x 6½"

From the blue solid, cut:

6 strips, 3" x 42"; crosscut *4 of the strips* into:
   2 pieces, 3" x 30½"
   2 pieces, 3" x 24"
   2 pieces, 3" x 12½"

From the red solid, cut:

8 strips, 3" x 42"; crosscut *5 of the strips* into:
   2 pieces, 3" x 36½"
   2 pieces, 3" x 30"
   2 pieces, 3" x 18½"

CUTTING THE REMAINING PIECES

1. Sew the remaining 10 white 4" x 42" strips together end to end to make one long strip. From the pieced strip, cut the following:

   2 pieces, 4" x 42½"

   2 pieces, 4" x 44½"

   2 pieces, 4" x 50½"

   1 piece, 4" x 60"

2. Sew the remaining five gray 3" x 42" strips together end to end to make one long strip. From the pieced strip, cut two pieces, 3" x 54", and two pieces, 3" x 42½".

3. Sew the remaining three red 3" x 42" strips together end to end to make one long strip. From the pieced strip, cut two pieces, 3" x 48".

MAKING THE BLOCKS

1. Sew the white 4" x 18" piece to the gray 3" x 18" piece along the long edges. Press the seam allowances open. Join the gray 3" x 6½" piece to the right edge of the unit. Press the seam allowances open.

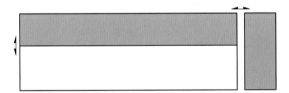

2. Referring to the illustration, sew the white, gray, blue, and red pieces to the previous unit in the order shown, alternating between the top and right sides of the unit.

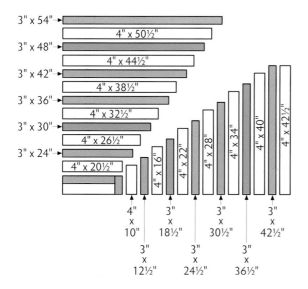

3. Repeat steps 1 and 2 to make a total of two blocks.

ASSEMBLING THE QUILT TOP

Refer to the quilt assembly diagram below to arrange the blocks and white 4" x 60" strip as shown. Sew the blocks and strip together. Press the seam allowances open.

FINISHING THE QUILT

Refer to "Quilt Finishing" on pages 14 and 15.

1. Piece the quilt backing so it is 6" longer and 6" wider than the quilt top.

2. Layer the quilt top with backing and batting; baste the layers together.

3. Quilt as desired. Quilting suggestion: I quilted this by alternating interlocking squares in the white and blue strips, Xs in the red strips, and zigzags in the gray strips. I used white, red, and gray thread so the quilting would add texture without adding contrast to the fabric.

4. Square up the quilt sandwich.

5. Bind the quilt with the white 2½"-wide strips.

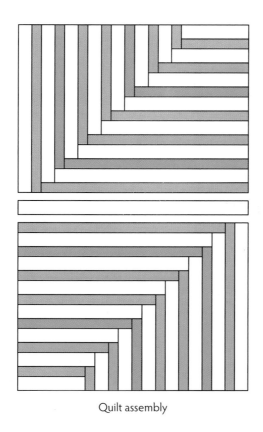

Quilt assembly

nursery
nap time

Expecting a baby is such an amazing and exciting time. With so many gorgeous fabrics to choose from, parents can truly design the nursery of their dreams. The following projects are the foundation of any beautiful nursery and can easily be customized to any taste.

GARDEN PATH CRIB QUILT

FINISHED QUILT: 40" x 55"

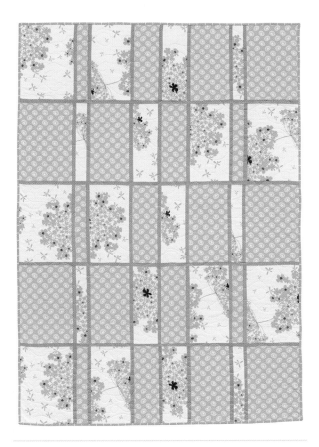

This lovely quilt is a great way to pair a large-scale print with a coordinating smaller print. Pick an accent color for the sashing, and you have a design that's both modern and classic.

MATERIALS

Yardage is based on 42"-wide fabric.

1⅛ yards of large-scale orange floral for rectangles

1⅛ yards of small-scale orange floral for rectangles

⅝ yard of gray solid for sashing

½ yard of orange stripe for binding

2⅞ yards of fabric for backing

46" x 61" piece of batting

MEASURE YOUR CRIB
Crib and mattress sizes vary slightly between manufacturers. The following projects are all designed around a crib measurement of 28" x 52". Be sure to double-check the measurements of your crib and mattress and make any size adjustments necessary.

CUTTING

From *each* of the large-scale and small-scale orange florals, cut:

3 strips, 11" x 42"; crosscut into:
    5 rectangles, 8" x 11" (10 total)
    5 rectangles, 6" x 11" (10 total)
    5 rectangles, 4" x 11" (10 total)
    5 rectangles, 2" x 11" (10 total)

From the gray solid, cut:

16 strips, 1" x 42"; crosscut into:
    35 rectangles, 1" x 11"
    4 strips, 1" x 40"

From the orange stripe, cut:

5 strips, 2½" x 42"

PIECING THE QUILT TOP

1. Lay out the large-scale and small-scale orange floral rectangles and the gray 1" x 11" rectangles into a horizontal row as shown. Sew the pieces together. Press the seam allowances open. Make five rows.

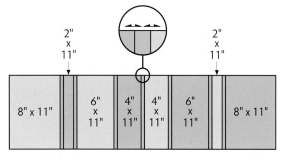

Make 5.

2. Refer to the quilt assembly diagram to alternately arrange the block rows and gray 1" x 40" strips as shown, reversing every other block row to create the design and matching seams from row to row. Sew the rows together. Press the seam allowances open.

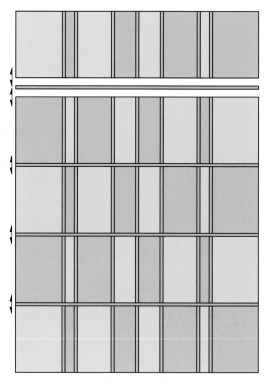

Quilt assembly

FINISHING THE QUILT

Refer to "Quilt Finishing" on pages 14 and 15.

1. Piece the quilt backing so it is 6" longer and 6" wider than the quilt top.

2. Layer the quilt top with backing and batting; baste the layers together.

3. Quilt as desired. Quilting suggestion: I quilted with whimsical, free-motion loops.

4. Square up the quilt sandwich.

5. Bind the quilt with the orange-stripe 2½"-wide strips.

TAILORED CRIB SKIRT

A crib skirt is a fun accent to any nursery. This modern and sleek design has a flat front, and because it's made from 54"-wide upholstery-weight fabric, the panels can be made in one piece. The crisp white border adds a classic element to the skirt.

MATERIALS

Yardage is based on 54"-wide home-decor fabric unless otherwise noted.

1⅞ yards of gray-print for skirt

⅔ yard of white solid twill for skirt border

1⅔ yards of 42"-wide white cotton or muslin for deck

CUTTING

From the gray print, cut:
2 pieces, 15" x 49"
2 pieces, 15" x 25"

From the white twill, cut:
2 pieces, 3½" x 49"
2 pieces, 3½" x 25"
8 pieces, 3½" x 17½"

From the white cotton or muslin, cut:
1 piece, 29" x 53"

MAKING THE CRIB SKIRT

Use ½"-wide seam allowances.

1. Sew a white 3½" x 49" piece to one long edge of a gray 15" x 49" piece. Refer to "Seam Finishes" (page 12) to finish the seam with your desired seam treatment. Press the seam allowances toward the white twill.

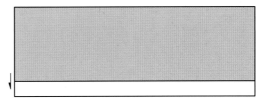

2. Sew white 3½" x 17½" pieces to the ends of the panel from step 1. Finish the seams and then press the seam allowances toward the white twill. Topstitch along the seams of the white pieces.

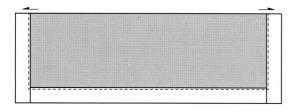

3. Repeat steps 1 and 2 to make a total of two side skirt panels.

4. Sew white 3½" x 25" pieces to one long edge of a gray 15" x 25" piece. Finish the seam. Press the seam allowances toward the white twill. Sew white 3½" x 17½" pieces to the ends of the panel. Finish the seams and press the seam allowances toward the white twill. Topstitch along the seams of the white pieces. Repeat to make a total of two end skirt panels.

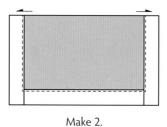

Make 2.

5. On both side panels and both end panels, press under the raw edge of the long white border pieces ½" twice to create a hem. Topstitch the hem in place. Repeat with the white end pieces.

6. Sew the side skirt panels to the long edges of the cotton or muslin 29" x 53" deck piece. Finish the seams and press the seam allowances toward the platform. Sew the end skirt panels to the short edges of the deck piece. Finish the seams and press the seam allowances toward the deck.

FITTED CRIB SHEET

FITS STANDARD CRIB MATTRESS (28" x 52")

Making crib sheets is fast and easy, and it's the perfect way to use exactly the right print to make the nursery complete. Making your own sheets is also an affordable way of using organic fabrics, like the Confetti print from Birch Fabrics.

MATERIALS

Yardage is based on 42"-wide fabric.

2⅛ yards of print

2 yards of ¼"-wide elastic

CUTTING

From the print, cut:

1 piece, 42" x 68"*

See "Measure Your Crib" on page 53 before cutting.

MAKING THE CRIB SHEET

1. Cut an 8" square from each corner of the sheet.

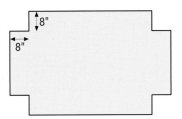

2. Pin the two sides of one corner together, wrong sides together, aligning the edges. Refer to "Flat Fell" (page 13) to sew a ½"-wide seam allowance and finish the seam. Repeat for the remaining three corners.

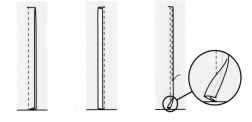

3. To make the casing for the elastic, press under ½" on all the raw edges. Press under the edges ½" again. Edgestitch as close as possible to the folded edge to allow as much room as possible for the elastic to be worked through the casing. Stop sewing 3" from the start of the stitches to allow enough room for the elastic to be inserted.

4. Place a safety pin through one end of the elastic. Use the pin to work the elastic through the casing, being careful not to twist the elastic.

5. Once the elastic is worked all the way through the casing, pull it out a couple of inches and sew the two ends of the elastic together. Stitch back and forth several times to reinforce the join.

6. Tug the sheet to pull the elastic back into the casing and then edgestitch the opening closed.

CRIB BUMPER

FINISHED BUMPER: 10" x 160"

MATERIALS

Yardage is based on 42"-wide fabric.

2⅞ yards of print for bumper

1 yard of coordinating solid for ties

1¼ yards of cotton batting

CUTTING

Be sure to measure the crib first in case there is a slight deviation in the perimeter of your quilt and the finished size of the bumper; adjust the pieces accordingly.

From the bumper print, cut:

8 strips, 11" x 42"

From the coordinating solid, cut:

7 strips, 2" x 42"; crosscut into 14 strips, 2" x 20"

From the batting, cut:

4 strips, 11" x 42"

PIECING THE BUMPER AND BATTING PANELS

1. Sew four bumper-print strips together end to end to make one long strip. Press the seam allowances open. Trim the piece to 11" x 161". Press the short ends under ½". Repeat to make a total of two bumper panels.

2. Butt the short ends of two batting pieces together and zigzag stitch over the pieces to join them. Repeat with the remaining batting pieces to make one long strip. Trim the piece to 11" x 160".

A crib bumper is a great accessory to any nursery and is particularly helpful in keeping little arms and legs from becoming stuck between the crib slats. This pattern uses cotton batting instead of thick bumper inserts, which means the bumper can't be used by little escape artists to stand on and climb out of the crib. This bumper features Birch's Wings of Love and Solid Shroom fabrics.

MAKING THE TIES

1. Press each solid 2" x 20" strip in half lengthwise, wrong sides together. Open up each strip and fold the long raw edges in to meet the center crease; press.

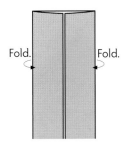

2. Press the short edges of each strip in ½". Fold the strip in half lengthwise along the original center crease; press. Topstitch along the open edges of each tie.

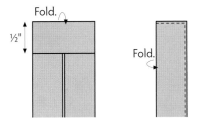

SAFETY TIP

According to the American Academy of Pediatrics, bumper pads carry a potential risk to babies' safety so use at your own discretion.

ASSEMBLING THE BUMPER

Use a ½"-wide seam allowance.

1. Fold the ties in half widthwise. Starting ½" from the left end of one bumper panel, pin a folded tie to the top and bottom edges of the panel, with the fold along the outer edge and the loose ends toward the center. Pin the remaining ties to the top and bottom edges of the bumper panel 26", 52", 80", 106", 132", and 159½" from the end of the bumper panel. Then layer the remaining bumper panel right sides together with this panel; the ties will be sandwiched between the layers. Place the batting strip on top of the panels. Tuck the short ends of the batting into the pressed-under ends of the bumper panel.

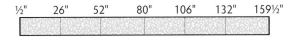

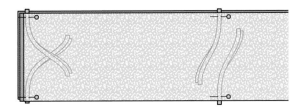

2. Sew the long edges together on each side of the bumper panel.

3. Clip the batting in the seam allowance to ⅛" to reduce bulk.

4. Turn the bumper right side out and press the seams. Topstitch along all of the edges, closing the short ends at the same time.

5. At the 52", 80", and 106" marks, sew a vertical line from the top to the bottom of the bumper. This will help the bumper fold at the crib corners.

6. Quilt the bumper, if desired.

nursery play time

A beautiful play mat and sweet plushies are the perfect presents for any new baby or expectant parent. They are bound to be favorites!

RIBBON LATTICE PLAY MAT

FINISHED PLAY MAT: 32" x 32" | FINISHED BLOCK: 8" x 8"

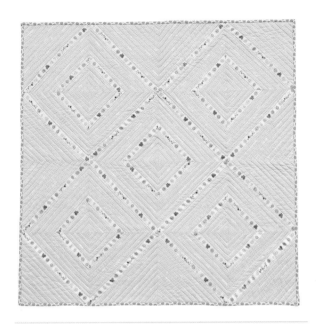

The play mat is made with pieced squares and appliquéd ribbons arranged to form a charming lattice pattern. Use a striped fabric, like Birch's Abacus Sun, cut on the bias to add a fun chevron detail.

MATERIALS

Yardage is based on 42"-wide fabric.

1⅛ yards of yellow print for blocks*

½ yard of pink polka dot for binding

1⅛ yards of fabric for backing

38" x 38" piece of cotton batting

10 yards of ¾"-wide grosgrain ribbon

If you're using a striped fabric that you want to cut on the bias, you'll need 1½ yards.

CUTTING

From the yellow print, cut:
16 squares, 8½" x 8½"

From the pink polka dot, cut:
4 strips, 2½" x 42"

From the ribbon, cut:
16 pieces, 12½" long
20 pieces, 7" long

MAKE IT A PHOTO SHOOT!

For baby's first year or two, take a monthly picture of your baby with the play mat and plushies. It's a great way to document your baby's growth and to turn these gorgeous, made-with-love projects into family heirlooms. The pictures make wonderful gifts, too.

MAKING THE BLOCKS

1. Draw a diagonal line from corner to corner on the *right* side of each yellow square. On four of the squares, mark the midpoint (4¼") on each side and draw diagonal lines from mark to mark on adjacent sides. On the remaining 12 squares, mark the midpoint on two adjacent sides and connect the marks with a diagonal line.

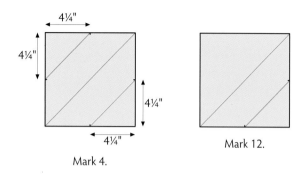

Mark 12.

Mark 4.

2. Center and pin a 12½" length of ribbon to the diagonal line that goes from corner to corner on each marked square. Center and pin a 7" length to the remaining marked lines on each square. If your ribbon is directional, be sure to keep the orientation of the ribbon consistent. Stitch close to the long edges on each length of ribbon. Trim the ribbon ends even with the edges of each square.

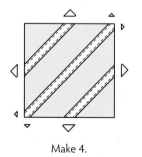

Make 4.

Make 12.

ASSEMBLING THE QUILT TOP

Refer to the quilt assembly diagram to arrange the blocks in four rows of four blocks each as shown, positioning the blocks with three ribbons in the quilt center. Sew the blocks in each row together. Press the seam allowances open. Sew the rows together. Press the seam allowances open.

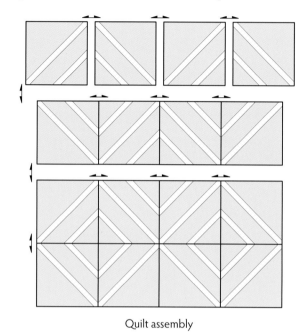

Quilt assembly

FINISHING THE QUILT

Refer to "Quilt Finishing" on pages 14 and 15.

1. Piece the quilt backing so it is 6" longer and 6" wider than the quilt top.

2. Layer the quilt top with backing and batting; baste the layers together.

3. Quilt as desired. I echo quilted the ribbons.

4. Square up the quilt sandwich.

5. Bind the quilt with the pink polka-dot 2½"-wide strips.

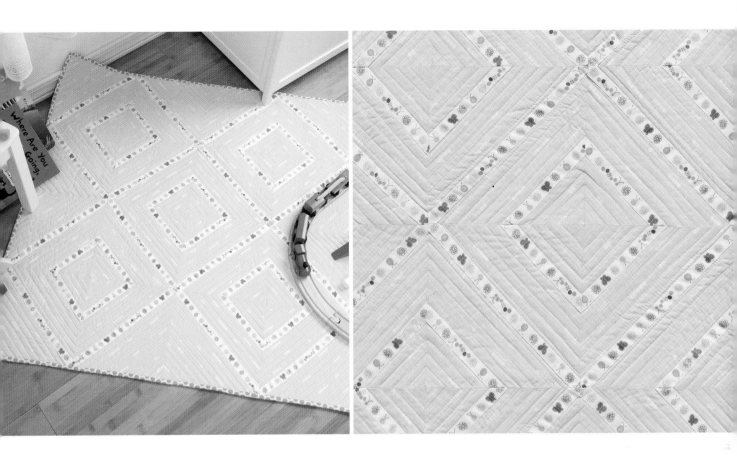

MODIFY IT

This design could easily be modified to use a print or solid fabric—or even rickrack—in place of the ribbon. Think how fun this would be to feature a fabric that's used elsewhere in your child's nursery or play room!

To use fabric, you'll need ⅝ yard of fabric and a ¾"-wide bias bar. Cut the fabric into nine strips, 2" wide. (These are not bias strips; simply cut across the grain. If you want to make bias strips to showcase a plaid, stripe, or other print on the diagonal, you'll need about 1 yard of fabric.) Sew the strips together end to end as you would for making binding. Then, fold the strips in half, wrong sides together, and stitch a scant ¼" from the raw edges. (Be sure to make the seam allowance scant so you can fit your bias bar in the tube after its sewn.)

At the ironing board, insert the bias bar into the tube and turn the tube so the seam is centered on one side of the bias bar. Press the seam allowances to one side while pressing the tube flat. Scoot the bias bar along the tube, pressing as you go until the entire tube is flat. Remove the bias bar and then press the fabric tube once more from the right side.

Now use the fabric tube just as you would the ribbon.

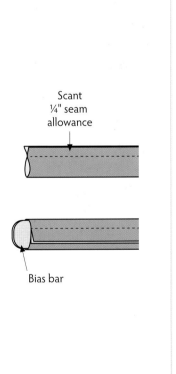

Scant ¼" seam allowance

Bias bar

PLUSHIE PENGUIN

FINISHED SIZE: 7" WIDE x 8" TALL

This sweet penguin is perfect for cuddling, either at home or on the go. He's bound to be a favorite with any child. Use a fun striped print, like Birch Fabrics' Abacus Teal, to dress him up a bit.

MATERIALS

Yardage is based on 42"-wide fabric.

⅓ yard of teal print for body and outer wings

8" x 10" piece of cream solid for body-front contrast

5" x 8" piece of blue polka-dot print for under wings

4" x 9" piece of orange solid for beak

3" x 6" piece of orange stripe for feet

2" x 2" square of black felt for eyes

Paper or pattern-making material

Cotton or polyester fiberfill

MAKING THE PENGUIN

Use ¼"-wide seam allowances and sew with right sides together.

1. Trace the patterns on pages 65–67 onto paper or pattern-making material, transferring all of the pattern markings; cut out the templates. Use the templates to cut out the pieces from the fabrics indicated. Transfer all of the pattern markings to the fabric pieces.

2. Using matching thread, machine sew the eyes to the right side of each front piece where indicated.

3. Sew each front piece to a side piece, extending the point of the side piece ¼" past the corner of the front piece. Sewing the curves is a bit tricky and takes patience. Reduce your stitch length and sew slowly. It also helps if you place the front piece on top of the side piece and use pins if necessary.

4. With the straight edges and seams aligned, sew the front pieces together.

5. Sew the two orange beak pieces together along both sides of the triangle, leaving the top open. Trim the seam allowances to a scant ⅛". Turn the beak right side out and press. Tuck the raw edges inside the beak ¼" and press.

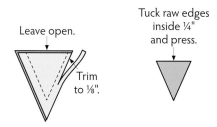

Leave open.

Tuck raw edges inside ¼" and press.

Trim to ⅛".

6. Using matching thread, slipstitch the beak to the face where indicated.

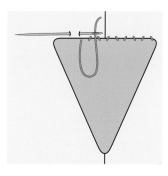

7. Place the front and back pieces together, matching the center-back mark to the center-front seam. Starting at the center mark, sew the pieces together in both directions, backstitching at the beginning and end of each seam.

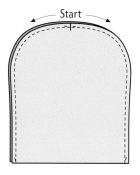

Start

8. Sew each teal wing to a polka-dot wing, leaving the straight edge open. Turn each wing right side out and tuck in the raw edges ¼"; press.

9. Machine stitch a wing to each side of the body where indicated.

10. Sew the feet pieces together, leaving the straight edge open. Trim the seam allowances to ⅛" along the front curves, and then turn the feet right side out. Press each foot, tucking in the raw edges ¼".

11. Sew the feet to the bottom where indicated.

12. Stitch the bottom piece to the body bottom raw edges, leaving a 2" opening on the back for turning. Turn the penguin right side out and stuff firmly with fiberfill. Slipstitch the opening closed.

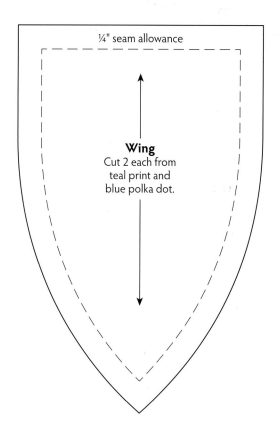

¼" seam allowance

Wing
Cut 2 each from teal print and blue polka dot.

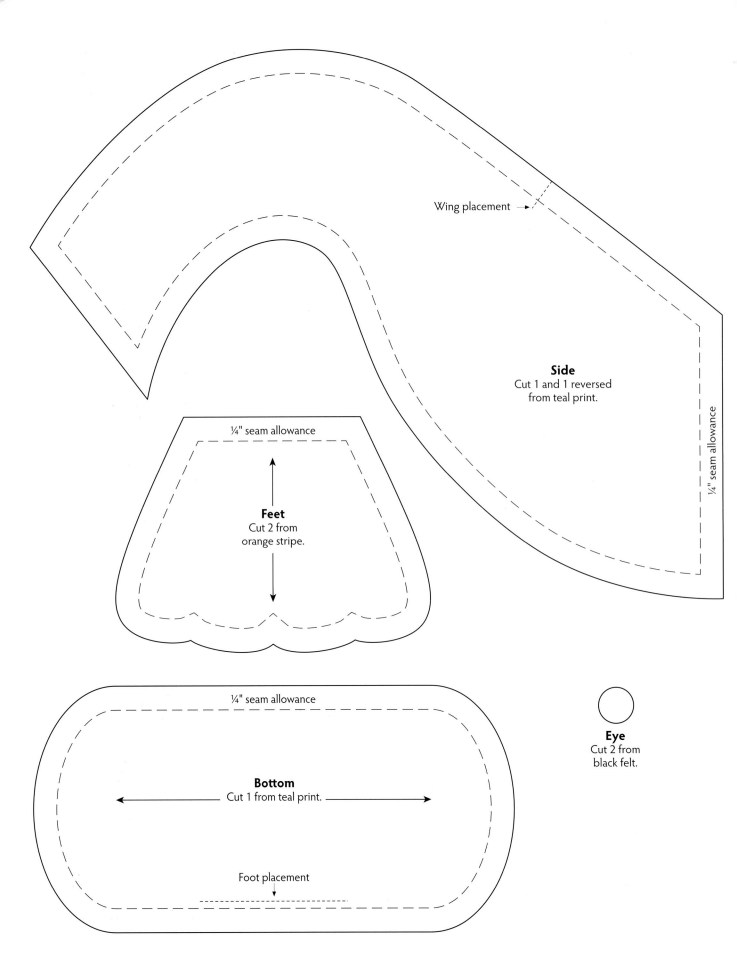

Wing placement →

Side
Cut 1 and 1 reversed
from teal print.

¼" seam allowance

¼" seam allowance

Feet
Cut 2 from
orange stripe.

¼" seam allowance

Bottom
Cut 1 from teal print.

Foot placement

Eye
Cut 2 from
black felt.

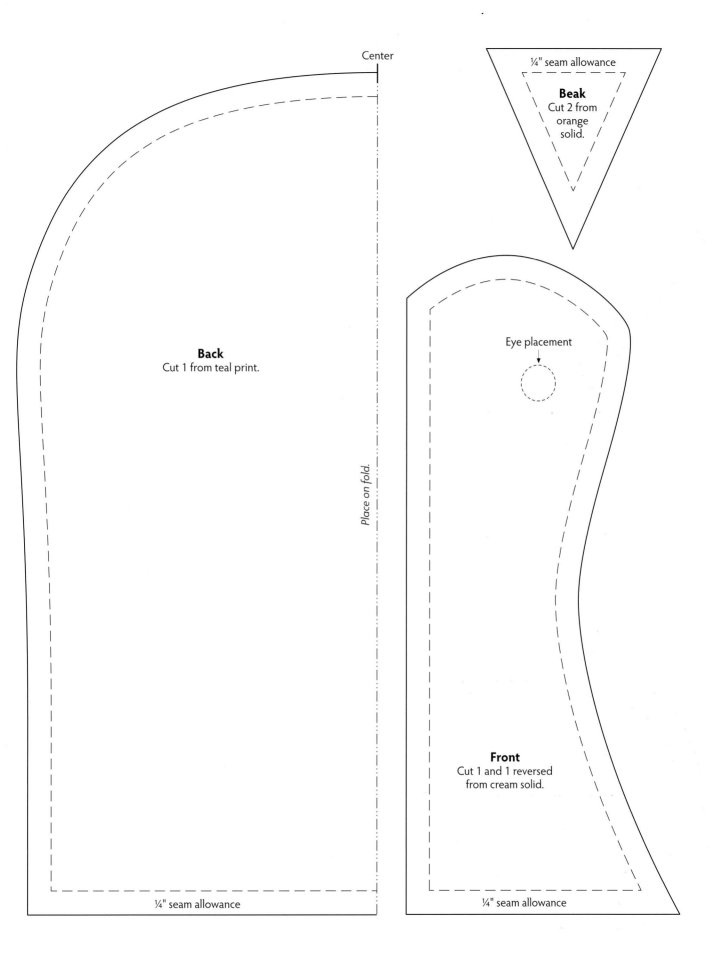

Center

¼" seam allowance

Beak
Cut 2 from
orange
solid.

Eye placement

Back
Cut 1 from teal print.

Place on fold.

Front
Cut 1 and 1 reversed
from cream solid.

¼" seam allowance

¼" seam allowance

OCTOPLUSHIE

FINISHED SIZE: 4" TALL x 7" DIAMETER; LEGS ARE 7" LONG

This little buddy is perfect for your favorite pair of small hands. The long limbs will make this an easy toy to grab on to and love, even for the smallest of hands. The felt eyes are securely sewn on, so there are no loose pieces to tear off. "Octoplushie" is made with Birch's Birdie Spokes Pool and Dottie Orange fabrics.

MATERIALS

Yardage is based on 42"-wide fabric.

½ yard of aqua print for body and upper limbs

¼ yard of orange polka dot for body bottom and under limbs

2" x 3" piece of white felt for eyes

2" x 2" square of black felt for eyes

Paper or pattern-making material

Cotton or polyester fiberfill

MAKING THE OCTOPUS

Use ¼"-wide seam allowances and sew with right sides together unless otherwise indicated.

1. Trace the patterns on pages 70 and 71 onto paper or pattern-making material, transferring all of the pattern markings; cut out the templates. Use the templates to cut out the pieces from the fabrics indicated. Transfer all of the pattern markings to the fabric pieces.

2. Using black thread, machine stitch each inner eye piece to an outer eye piece where indicated. Using white thread, sew the joined eye pieces to one body piece where indicated.

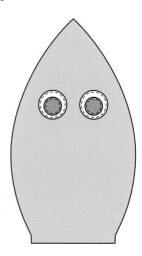

3. Sew two body pieces together along one curved edge. Finger-press the seam allowances open. Repeat to make a total of three pairs. Sew the pairs together to make one continuous piece. Press the seam allowances open. Turn the body right side out.

Make 3.

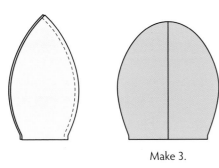

4. To make the limbs, sew each aqua limb piece to an orange polka-dot limb piece, leaving the straight end open and a 2" opening on one long edge. Trim the seam allowances along the bottom curve of each piece to a scant ⅛".

5. Turn each leg right side out and press, tucking in ¼" along the opening on the side of the leg.

6. With the aqua fabrics facing each other, pin the limbs to the body, spacing them approximately ¾" apart. Using a ⅛" seam allowance, stitch the limbs in place, going over the stitching a second time to reinforce the seam.

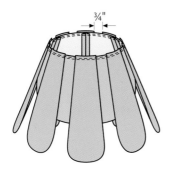

7. Turn the octopus wrong side out and tuck the legs inside the body.

8. Fold the bottom piece in half vertically and horizontally; finger-press the creases.

9. Pin the bottom piece to the bottom raw edges of the body, matching one crease to opposite seams and positioning the other crease ends midway between the remaining seams. Stitch, leaving a 2" opening for turning.

Leave 2" opening.

10. Turn the octopus right side out and stuff the body and legs firmly with fiberfill. Slipstitch the openings closed.

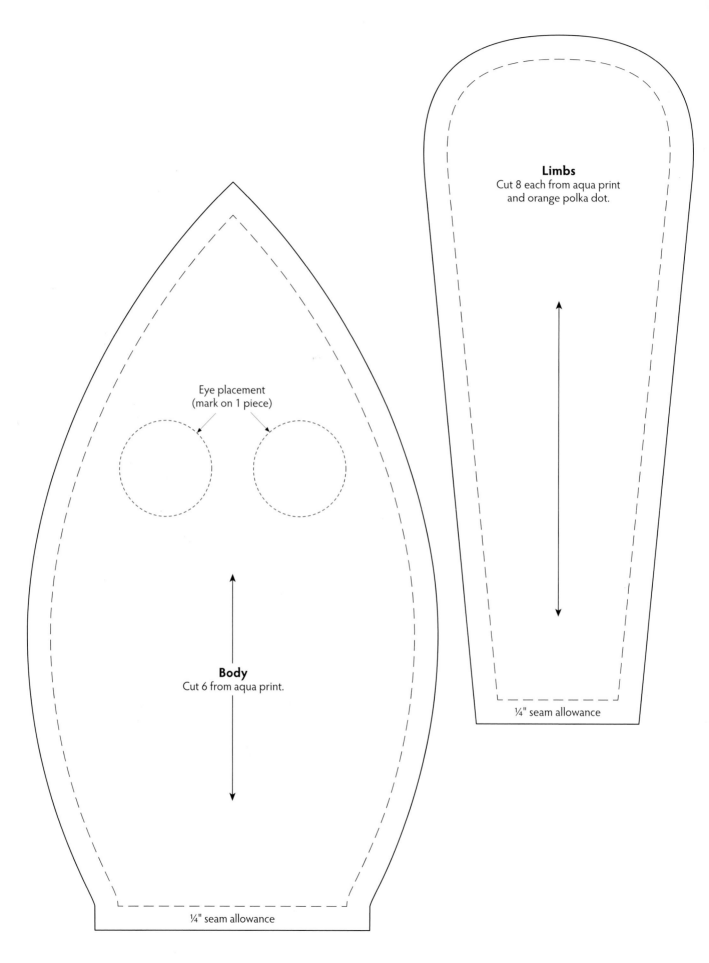

Limbs
Cut 8 each from aqua print
and orange polka dot.

¼" seam allowance

Eye placement
(mark on 1 piece)

Body
Cut 6 from aqua print.

¼" seam allowance

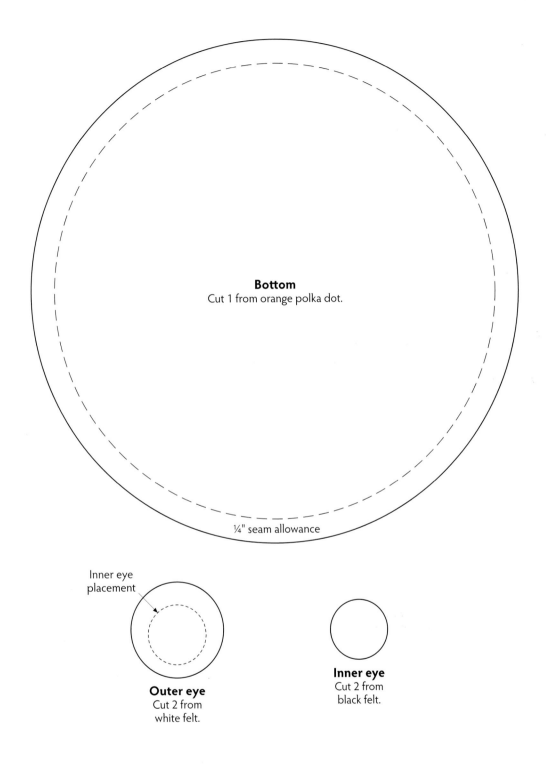

Bottom
Cut 1 from orange polka dot.

¼" seam allowance

Inner eye
placement

Outer eye
Cut 2 from
white felt.

Inner eye
Cut 2 from
black felt.

out and about

Love of good design and beautiful things doesn't have to be limited to the inside of the home. Here are two great projects for when you're out and about. The picnic quilt will be sure to get a lot of love, and the tote bag is a perfect, stylish way of carrying your picnic lunch, or for shopping at your favorite farmers' market.

THE BEE'S KNEES PICNIC QUILT

FINISHED QUILT: 59" x 59" | FINISHED BLOCK: 19½" x 19½"

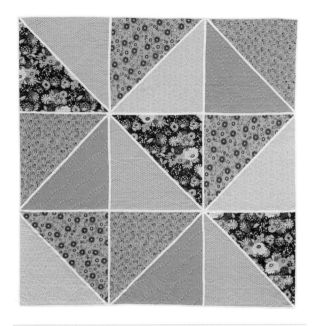

Warm weather is all about parks, picnics, concerts, and enjoying the outdoors. What better way to do that than with this gorgeous picnic quilt? The design is fresh and not too fussy, but it will be sure to make your next outdoor adventure all the more special.

MATERIALS

Yardage is based on 42"-wide fabric.

⅔ yard *each* of 6 assorted green florals for blocks

1¼ yards of white solid for sashing and binding

4 yards of fabric for backing

68" x 68" piece of batting

CUTTING

From *each* of the 6 green florals, cut:

2 squares, 20" x 20" (12 total); cut in half diagonally to make 4 triangles (24 total; you'll have 6 left over)

From the white solid, cut:

19 strips, 1" x 42"; crosscut *15 of the strips* into:
    9 strips, 1" x 32"
    6 strips, 1" x 20"
7 strips, 2½" x 42"

MAKING THE BLOCKS

Use ¼"-wide seam allowances and sew with right sides together.

1. Fold each white 1" x 32" strip in half crosswise, wrong sides together, and finger-press the fold.

2. Select two different green triangles. Fold each triangle in half along the long edge and finger-press the fold at the edge.

3. With the center marks aligned, sew the white strip to the long edge of one of the triangles. Press the seam allowances open.

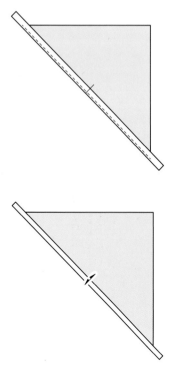

4. With the center marks aligned, sew the remaining triangle to the remaining long edge of the white strip. Press the seam allowances open.

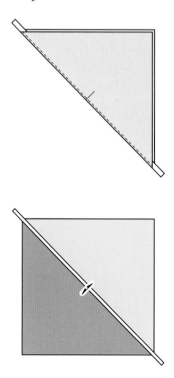

5. Square up the block to 20" square, keeping the white strip centered.

6. Repeat steps 2–5 to make a total of nine blocks.

ASSEMBLING THE QUILT TOP

1. Refer to the quilt assembly diagram below to lay out the blocks in three rows of three blocks and two white 1" x 20" sashing strips, alternating the blocks and sashing strips. Sew the pieces in each row together. Press the seam allowances open.

2. Sew the remaining four white 1" x 42" strips together end to end to make one long strip. From the pieced strip, cut two horizontal sashing strips, 1" x 59".

3. Sew the block rows together, inserting a horizontal sashing strip between the rows. Press the seam allowances open.

FINISHING THE QUILT

Refer to "Quilt Finishing" on pages 14 and 15.

1. Piece the quilt backing so it is 6" longer and 6" wider than the quilt top.

2. Layer the quilt top with backing and batting; baste the layers together.

3. Quilt as desired. Quilting suggestion: I free-motion quilted the quilt shown with my favorite whimsical loops.

4. Square up the quilt sandwich.

5. Bind the quilt with the white 2½"-wide strips.

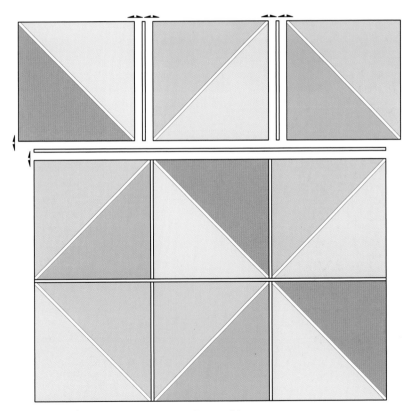

Quilt assembly

FARMERS' MARKET TOTE

>>

This classic tote is made out of heavyweight French ticking, although you could substitute pillow ticking or a home-decor fabric. The pocket cut on the bias and the pop of green webbing for the straps make this the perfect bag for stylish picnics and shopping.

MATERIALS

1⅔ yards of 32"-wide ticking stripe for outer bag and lining

1⅛ yards of 1¾"-wide green webbing

100/16 sewing-machine needle

Jeans or topstitching thread

Template plastic (optional)

CUTTING

From the ticking, cut:
2 rectangles, 19½" x 31"

From the remaining ticking, cut *on the bias:*
1 rectangle, 7" x 9"

From the webbing, cut:
2 pieces, 18" long

SHAPING THE BAG BODY

1. Fold a 19½" x 31" rectangle in half to make a piece 19½" x 15½".

2. Make a mark 1" in from both short edges of the piece along the top of the bag. Using a ruler, cut a diagonal line from the 1" mark to the bottom corner on both sides as shown.

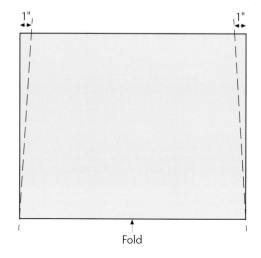

Fold

3. Cut out a 1½" x 2" rectangle from both bottom corners.

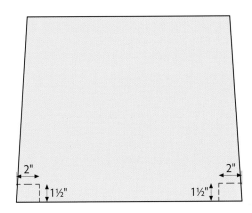

4. Trace the curve template (page 79) onto template plastic or paper and cut it out. Center the template along the top of the bag, 4" from each side. Trace around the template and then cut out the shape.

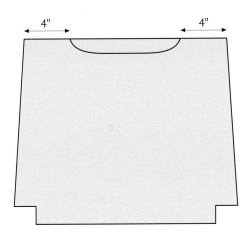

5. Repeat steps 1–4 with the remaining ticking rectangle for the lining.

MAKING THE POCKET

1. Press under the two short sides and one long side of the ticking 7" x 9" bias rectangle ½". Clip the excess fabric at the corners to reduce bulk, and then press each side under ½" again.

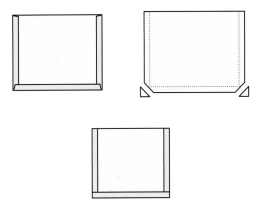

2. Press the remaining long edge under ½" twice and then topstitch close to the first folded edge.

3. Center the pocket on one side of the outer bag, 2¾" from the curved top edge. Topstitch the pocket to the bag along the pocket side and bottom edges.

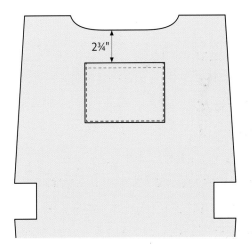

ASSEMBLING THE BAG

Use ½"-wide seam allowances and sew with right sides together unless otherwise indicated.

1. Sew the outer bag side seams together. Press the seam allowances open.

2. Pinch a side seam and the bottom of the bag together, centering the side seam. Sew ½" from the raw edges. Repeat with the opposite side seam.

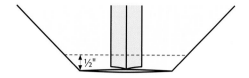

3. Repeat steps 1 and 2 with the lining pieces, but leave a 6" opening on one side for turning the bag later.

4. Turn the outer bag piece right side out.

5. Pin the raw edges of a webbing strip to the top edge of the outer bag ½" from the curve. Sew the straps in place using a ¼" seam allowance. Repeat on the other side of the outer bag.

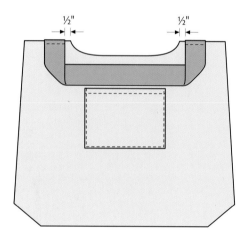

6. Insert the outer bag into the lining, right sides together. Pin the pieces together along the top edges, matching the side seams. Sew the pieces together, following the curves on each side.

7. Turn the bag right side out through the opening in the side seam of the lining. Slipstitch the opening closed.

8. Push the lining into the interior of the outer bag, pushing out the corners. Topstitch along the top edge of the bag.

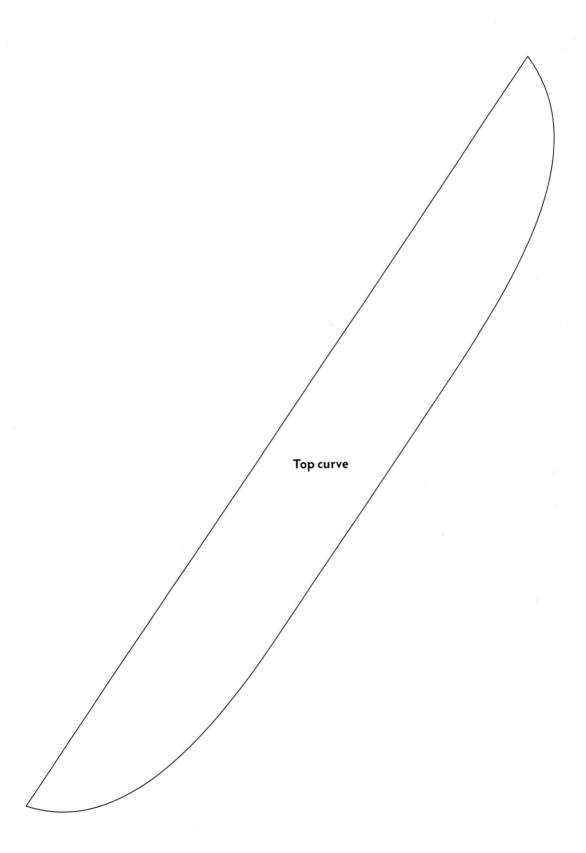

Top curve

ABOUT THE AUTHOR

PHOTO BY JEANNE ELLENBY

Melissa Lunden is a lifelong lover of all things crafty. Her passion for sewing and fabric has led to her starting her own sewing-pattern company, Lunden Designs. Her work has been featured in multiple magazines and at the International Quilt Market. She currently lives in Portland, Oregon, with her husband and daughter. You can visit her website at www.lundendesigns.com.